Overcon Shyne  Confident and Outgoing

Written by: Beau Norton

CEO & Owner of:

Health & Happiness Foundation

My Free Gift to You

To help speed up your personal transformation, I have made an affirmation audio track that you can listen to at your convenience. This mp3 uses binaural beat technology, which helps the suggestions penetrate the depths of your subconscious mind where they will begin to shift your beliefs to ones that will better serve you on your journey.

If you are interested, go to the following web address:

healthandhappinessfoundation.com/101-affirmations-for-success-audio

Introduction

Hi, my name is Beau. For a large portion of my life, I suffered from chronic anxiety and a major lack of self-confidence, and this book is going to be about the methods I used to overcome my crippling fears and insecurities in a short amount of time. Understanding a few key principles and taking the time to do a few simple daily activities was all it took for me to overcome my social anxiety and shyness. I know how it feels to be lonely and isolated, and I know how damaging a lack of self-confidence can be, and so that is why I am writing this book for you – in hopes that you can turn your life around like I did and go on to live a happier and more fulfilling life. You deserve it.

Understanding Anxiety

If you want to eliminate anxiety from your life and overcome your fears and insecurities, it's important that you first go within yourself to really examine the underlying causes of your condition. The reason I was able to overcome much of my shyness and social anxiety was because I took the time to study myself on a deeper level and really be honest about my problems. If you are unwilling to face your problems head on, you will never be able to make massive progress in your life, and so this chapter is going to be about how you can begin to understand and accept yourself one hundred percent while coming face to face with your deepest fears and insecurities. From there, making positive changes becomes much easier.

Let emotion flow through you rather than take you over…

Anxiety and stress manifest as uncomfortable emotions within the body. Emotion is simply a form of energy. If measured, you could see that different emotions actually vibrate at different frequencies and have different electrical charges to them. Positive emotions like joy vibrate at a higher frequency, while negative emotions like anger vibrate at a much lower frequency. All emotion is just energy vibrating at a particular frequency, and so learning to "raise your vibration" is an important skill to learn. To explain the science behind this would require me to delve into the field of quantum physics, but I won't bore you with that. What I really want you to get from this is the notion that anxiety can in fact be turned into joy by doing a few simple things. Let me explain.

How exactly can you raise your vibration and turn anxiety into joy, or at least a more positive emotion? It's quite simple really, but it takes some practice. What you need to learn to do is let the energy of the emotion you are feeling flow through you instead of becoming trapped inside you. Have you noticed that when you are experiencing anxiety, you feel tense and constricted? This is due to the energy of your emotions becoming trapped in your musculature. When the muscles become tense, stress and anxiety increases, which causes the muscles to become even tenser. This cycle often repeats itself until the person removes their self from the stressful situation or has a panic attack, both of which are ways to release the excess energy that has become trapped in the body. But if you want to live your life to the fullest, neither of those two things are an option. You must learn how to face situations head on and deal with your negative emotions in a healthy way. In the following paragraphs, I will give you an extremely effective way to release the excess energy of negative emotions, raise your vibration, and thus turn anxiety into a more positive experience within a matter of moments.

Positive emotions such as joy naturally flow through your body, because you are more relaxed and "in the moment" as some would say. Anxiety and stress, however, causes tension in the body and doesn't allow the emotional energy to flow through you. So, to create joy from anxiety, all you have to do is let the energy in your body flow more freely. To do this effectively, focus your attention on the feeling within your body.

When we become stressed or anxious, our natural tendency is to immediately start thinking and rationalizing in our minds, but this is *very* counterproductive if you want to feel relaxed and at ease. Whenever you find yourself in a stressful situation and notice yourself getting caught up in the process of thinking, immediately shift your attention to the sensations in your body. *Feel* your emotions (If you are in a social setting, you may need to remove yourself from it for a moment to calm yourself and try this, however, it is also important that you learn to do this in the heat of the moment). Try to pinpoint the places in your body where you feel tension. Start by feeling the sensation in your feet and work your way up to your head. If you come across an area of your body that is tense, consciously relax it and continue feeling every body part until you have relaxed all your muscles to the best of your ability. If you are still feeling a strong sense of anxiety or tension, then you may just need to practice this more often. In any case, do not worry, because I have many more tips and strategies for you.

When you shift your attention from thinking to feeling the sensations in your body, you break the cycle of negative thinking and become present to the moment. "Thinking" is essentially the opposite of being present to the moment, while "feeling" naturally brings you into the present moment. Thinking often results in stress and anxiety, while 'feeling' naturally brings you into a calm and relaxed state. This is why getting into the habit of *feeling* your emotions is so important. As you get better at sensing emotional energy and tension in your body, you will notice that you can more easily release that built up energy and get into a positive state. By becoming more present to the moment, you relax your body and mind, and this allows negative emotions to flow through you and disappear.

The one thing I believe is extremely important for anyone who suffers from anxiety to understand is that anxiety is a direct result of excessive and negative thinking. In the next chapter, I will explain how you can stop the habit of negative thinking, but what I hope that you get from this chapter is the idea that the process of thinking can be bypassed altogether by simply getting more in touch with your feelings. Negative thinking cannot control your life when you are living through your body instead of your mind. Thinking is a useful tool in certain situations, but it serves very little purpose when all you want to do is feel comfortable and relaxed in social situations. The person who is most relaxed and present to the moment (living through the body) is usually the most charismatic and attractive person in the room, while the one who is nervous or anxious (caught up in thinking) is usually the one who has little to say and finds it difficult to connect with people. The first step to overcoming your shyness and/or social anxiety is to practice getting out of your head and into your body by becoming aware of your emotions and placing your attention on the sensations that you experience.

What it really boils down to is living in the moment. When you experience the increased joy and satisfaction that comes from being able to stop, or at least slow down your thoughts and live through your five senses, a whole new world of possibilities opens up for you. You will realize that your thoughts don't have to have so much control over you, and you will start to see how beautiful life really is. If you would like a complete guide on how to live in the moment and relieve stress or emotional pain, I highly recommend you pick up a copy of Eckhart Tolle's book "The Power of Now."

Being the shy kid is no fun. I know, because I've been there. However, I'm here to tell you that you can overcome that like I did and go on to live a much greater life than you ever thought possible. With a little practice and hard work, you will be well on your way to extreme confidence and a great social life.

For the time being, it's important that you accept yourself and all of your flaws. As they say, "what you resist persists," so don't fight against your emotions or try to stop them from happening – let them flow through you and naturally be released.

Shyness and social anxiety is very common. Know that you are not alone, but also know that you do not have to be bound by these minor flaws of yours. With a little persistence, you will be well on your way to living the life you dream of. There are no limits to what you can achieve.

In this chapter, you learned about how to get in touch with your emotions and let them flow through you rather than become trapped in your body. In this next chapter, I'm going to teach you how to reverse any negative thinking patterns that you may have so that your thoughts don't cause you so much stress and anxiety in the first place.

Reframing Personal Beliefs

Essentially, all of our actions are controlled by the way we think about ourselves. In other words, *we become who we imagine ourselves to be.* Yes, I said *imagine,* because a personal belief is simply a story that we make up in our heads and tell ourselves over and over again until we begin to believe it and act as if it were true. This is important to understand, because changing the way you behave in the world requires a change in the way that you view yourself. If you are stuck in thinking "I am a shy person that has no friends," then your actions will always be that of a shy person with no friends. A belief such as this is not the *truth*, it is only a story that you tell yourself, and it limits you greatly. The good news is that you have the power to *choose the story* that you tell yourself, and therefore you have the power to *choose who you become*!

Restructure your thoughts so they serve you instead of defeat you…

Firstly, understand that the only difference between you and some of the greatest people that have ever lived is the *thoughts and beliefs* that you have about yourself. You are just as amazing and just as capable as the greatest to ever live, you just may not have cultivated that belief yet. In order to become everything that you wish to be, you must change your current beliefs to the beliefs of the type of person who you would like to be. Do you think that a confident and outgoing person has thoughts like "I'm shy and have no friends"? Of course not. A confident person's thoughts may be more like "I am a likable person that people look up to and admire." To become a more confident and outgoing person, you will need to instill more positive beliefs such as this into your mind.

Now, you may be thinking "but all the evidence points to the fact that I'm shy and insecure, so how am I supposed to think confidently?" Surely, it is easier said than done, but the thought restructuring exercise I'm about to teach you will make it possible for you to slowly rid yourself of the negative beliefs that do not serve you and replace them with positive, empowering beliefs that motivate and uplift you.

For maximum results, use the following thought restructuring methods in conjunction with everything mentioned in the first chapter:

As you go through your day, it is likely that you spend most of your time thinking about anything and everything. While this is very normal, it is not a very effective way to make changes to your beliefs and attitude. Most of our thoughts are automatic and habitual, so changing them can be very difficult, however, if you practice getting into your body and feeling your emotions as discussed in the previous chapter, changing your negative thoughts to positive ones becomes much easier. When you *feel more* and *think less*, you suddenly become much more aware of all your negative thoughts. When you are busy feeling your emotions, a thought that pops into your head will capture your attention much more easily than if you were just thinking all day long non-stop. For this reason, it is important to practice getting in touch your feelings and emotions every single day. The better you get at that, the more aware you will become of your thoughts and the more power you will have to change those thoughts into ones that better serve you.

Let's say that you are very good now at living through your body and staying in touch with your emotions, but you still have negative beliefs about yourself that limit you in your personal and social life. Perhaps every now and then, while you are busy focusing on the feelings within your body, you notice the little voice in your head say something like "I'm so lame, I can't even hold a conversation for more than a minute." This was a limiting belief that I once had and struggled to overcome, so that is why I am using it as an example. In any case, this situation is a good one because you are now more aware of these types of thoughts, whereas you may have been too busy *thinking* to ever recognize them before. So now you've noticed this negative thought of yours and see it clearly. This is good news. This is where change occurs.

The moment you become extremely aware of a negative thought that comes into your mind, immediately say to yourself "DELETE!" Then take three deep breaths and repeat a positive affirmation to yourself three times. An affirmation is simply a statement about yourself worded in the present tense. The process may go something like this: You think to yourself "I'm so lame" and catch yourself thinking this. At this point, you realize that this is a negative thought, so you immediately say "DELETE!" (Out loud or in your head). This interrupts the negative thought pattern and prevents it from repeating. Next, you take three deep breaths to further interrupt and cancel out the negative thought. After this, you should repeat a positive thought to yourself three times in order to program yourself to automatically think positively after becoming aware of a negative thought. So, you say to yourself something that you would like to be true about yourself like "I'm confident, courageous, and outgoing." Say this three times. Even if you don't believe you are confident, courageous and outgoing, you are essentially programming your brain to believe that you are by repeating it often. If you can consistently catch yourself thinking self-defeating thoughts and then immediately interrupt that thought process using the method above, you will slowly but surely transform your mindset into that of a more positive person. Being positive and optimistic is a key component in the process of becoming more confident and outgoing.

This method may seem a little odd to you, but I assure you that it works. It is by no means a quick fix, but it will effectively instill in you the positive beliefs that are required for you to live a positive life. I began to use this exact method a long time ago, because I was extremely depressed and desperate to make a change. I can honestly say that catching my negative thoughts before they took control of me and repeating the positive affirmations to myself every day made a tremendous difference in my life. Today I am very optimistic and more confident than I've ever been, and most of my transformation happened through the very methods I have explained to you in these first two chapters. I am confident that you will see major positive changes in your life if you use this information and apply it consistently.

By restructuring your beliefs into more positive ones, you will experience much less stress and anxiety in your life, because it is our thoughts that create our emotions. Creating positive thoughts will create positive emotions, and every area of your life will benefit as a result of doing so. Remember, your thoughts and beliefs are just a story that you tell yourself, and you are ultimately in control of what story you choose to tell yourself. Those negative and limiting beliefs no longer serve you. You were destined for great things. The person you dream of being is already within you and is just waiting to be unleashed. Start thinking like that person and you will have no choice but to become that person.

Autosuggestion

It is sometimes difficult to have a level of awareness that allows you to effectively replace old thoughts with new ones, so I would like to offer you a simpler method that can be used from the comfort of your own home. This method is called autosuggestion, sometimes referred to as the use of affirmations. Autosuggestion is the repetition of certain thoughts with the intention of changing your core beliefs and attitudes. Essentially, our behavior is just a product of our underlying beliefs, and autosuggestion is an effective method for changing those beliefs and therefore changing our behavior to that of which we desire.

The use of autosuggestion is quite straightforward. You choose a thought that you would like to make a reality and repeat that thought over and over until your subconscious mind accepts it as truth. For example, you might choose to believe the thought, "I am confident and outgoing." By repeating that thought over and over while simultaneously visualizing yourself acting as if you were in fact confident and outgoing, you give your subconscious the message, "I want to accept this statement as true." With enough repetition and emotion, you will have no choice but to make that belief a reality. The method is simple to implement, but it takes consistency and discipline to instill the belief in your mind so it sticks and becomes part of who you are, or rather *who you think you are*.

To make this process easier for you, I have created an audio track with 50 empowering affirmations for you. You can always choose to create your own affirmations that suit you and your goals, but this audio I have made will at least give you an idea of how to use autosuggestion for your benefit. You can get the audio for free by signing up at:

healthandhappinessfoundation.com

Listen to the affirmations daily, preferably while in a relaxed state of mind. Right before you go to sleep would be ideal. The affirmations are set to relaxing meditation music so that the messages are more easily absorbed into your subconscious mind.

Remember that any thought repeated enough times becomes a belief, and beliefs are the basis from which you operate in the world. Change the thoughts that you feed your mind, and you have no choice but to change your attitude and behavior. You can in fact go from shy and insecure to extremely confidence simply by using the power of repetition through the use of autosuggestion.

Not only is it important to consciously feed your mind positive thoughts, but it is also important to be aware of what you allow other people and influences to feed your mind. Make sure to avoid negative influence such as violent TV programs, video games, negative people, etc. Everything you allow to enter into your mind has an effect on who you become.

Getting Your Life in Order

Before really diving into the social world and practicing your skills, it is a good idea to have a solid foundation to fall back on just in case you become overwhelmed. The last thing you want is to have a massive amount of stress put on you from getting out of your comfort zone only to go home to a messy house, crumbling relationship, financial crisis, or anything else that may cause you additional stress.

Overcoming shyness and social anxiety will require you to get a little uncomfortable at times, but if you have the rest of your life in order, you will have a much easier time focusing on and improving your social skills. If you have other worries in the back of your mind, you will not have as much mental clarity, and practicing your social skills will cause you much more stress than it would if you were to have the rest of your life well-organized.

This book is meant to give you steps to take that make the process of overcoming your fears and insecurities simple and as easy as possible. When one area of your life is disorganized, it tends to negatively affect all the other areas of your life as well, and so I think that it's a great idea to have a place of comfort and security in your life before you go out and face the social world head-on. In this chapter, I'm going to give you a few simple steps that you can take to get organized and feel more confident about the general direction in which your life is headed.

Set goals and define your life's purpose...

Having goals and working towards them will give you a strong sense of direction in your life, and this is important for many reasons. Firstly, it gives your life new meaning and motivates you to make steady progress in your life. When you begin to see yourself improving and getting closer to your goals as the weeks go by, your confidence will increase in proportion to the amount of progress you make. With this increased confidence, all the other challenges in your life will seem far less challenging. Your shyness and social anxiety will naturally be lessened by this increase in your self-esteem.

Another advantage of setting goals and working towards them is that it takes your attention away from your problems and puts it on something more positive and inspiring. If you find yourself worrying a lot, perhaps you need some bigger goals to focus on. Worrying can create a cycle of negative thinking, which is the opposite of what you want. The more time you allocate to achieving your goals, the less time you will have to spend worrying and stressing out about your problems. When you are making progress in your life and spending less time worrying, your level of happiness and confidence increases greatly, and these are things that will support you in all areas of your life.

I suggest that you take a few hours of your time to write down *in detail* your short and long-term goals. The simple act of writing your goals down on paper greatly increases the chances of you achieving those goals. With your life properly planned out, you will unburden your mind of all the stress that comes from not knowing where your life is headed.

Get your finances in order and your living space organized…

Money can be a huge stressor in today's society. Although I believe that money is not something any of us should worry so much about, considering most of us have *more* than enough, the fact that it causes a lot of stress and worrying cannot be denied. For this reason, it is important to have a financial plan that ensures you will have enough money to survive and pay the bills. If you are in debt, set up a plan that allows you to pay it off as quickly as possible. Create the habit of saving at least 10% of every paycheck. You will feel much more at peace when you know that you have money in the bank and all your bills taken care of. Peace of mind + less stress = more happiness and a greater ability to tackle the rest of your problems.

Another way to greatly reduce your stress is by keeping a clean home and work space. Material clutter can easily cause you to feel cluttered mentally as well.

When you come home after a stressful day, the last thing you want to see is a cluttered or messy home. Home should be a place to relax and unwind, and a messy environment is often not the greatest place for doing that. If you are naturally unorganized like me, then this may be more difficult for you, so perhaps a good strategy for you would be to set aside one hour every week to focus on cleaning and organizing. This should be sufficient enough to maintain a relatively clean and organized home.

You may be wondering what all this has to do overcoming shyness or social anxiety. The reason I mention the importance of things like organization and life planning is because these are things that can greatly reduce your overall stress levels. Minimizing stress is essential for making positive changes of any kind. The less stress you have to deal with, the more energy you will have to put towards your higher priorities, such as improving your social life. If you suffer from social anxiety, then interacting with other people is initially going to be extremely stressful for you, but you will see much greater improvements and faster results when you don't have to worry about coming home to a messy house or how you're going to pay rent next month. By organizing your life first, you ensure that every step on your journey of personal development is a more enjoyable one.

Practicing Your Social Skills at Home

Before throwing yourself into stressful social situations, it is a good idea to build up as much confidence as you possibly can, and that's why I recommend practicing your social skills by yourself before practicing them in front of people. There are a number of ways you can practice your social skills without actually having to socialize with anyone. In this chapter, I'm going to give you a couple ideas for ways to increase the confidence you have in your ability to effectively communicate.

Film yourself talking…

For someone who suffers from social anxiety, something as simple as talking in front of a camera can be extremely difficult, but it is actually one of the best ways for someone to practice their social skills outside of a social setting. If you can become confident in front of a camera, you will naturally become more confident in your ability to communicate and socialize with other people.

Use a digital camera or webcam to record yourself talking about various topics. Pick something that you know a little bit about, turn on your camera, and record yourself talking about that topic for at least five minutes. Practice this with multiple different topics. The goal should be for you to get to the point where you can talk about any topic for five to ten minutes without stopping. The better you get at conveying your ideas in front of a camera, the better you will get at conveying these same ideas to other people. If you suffer from social anxiety, you may find it hard to carry on a conversation for more than a few minutes. If you practice speaking about different topics in front of the camera, when it comes to carrying on a conversation with someone, you will have more to talk about and will have an easier time conveying your ideas and getting your message across. This will lead to an increased ability to make friends and communicate with people on a deeper level.

After you record yourself talking about a certain topic, go back and watch the recording. Listen to the way you speak and notice your body language. Do you talk with confidence and conviction, or do you sound quiet and unsure of yourself? Do you hold your head up and look directly into the camera when you talk, or do you fidget and look around? Pay close attention to these things and make an effort to improve your way of speaking and body language in each video. The way you look and sound on camera is likely similar to the way you do when you speaking to others. Fixing these issues at home will give you the extra confidence you need when going out to meet new people. When you can confidently speak in front of a camera, all you have to do is maintain that same attitude when you speak to others. Face to face interaction is what will help you develop your social skills the most, but speaking in front of a camera is a great way for you to build up a to a level of confidence that makes socializing with people much easier.

Word games…

Another great way to fine-tune your social skills at home is by playing word games. The goal of these games is to improve your ability to speak about absolutely anything at all and to make your conversations flow more naturally. Here is an example of one of these games that you can try at home (speaking out loud):

Yesterday I went to the bank. The bank got robbed a long time ago. You know what else happened a long time ago? Dinosaurs. Jurassic Park is my favorite movie. Every once in a while, I will just lay in bed all day and watch movies back to back. It makes me feel lazy and worthless when I do that. When I feel lazy and worthless, I like to exercise because it makes me feel better. I feel much better when I'm productive. I'm more productive when I'm alone. Being alone helps me relax….

Okay, now this is just an example of what I might say to myself if I was practicing this word game. Do you see how every sentence relates to the one before it? That is the only rule for this game. Sometime when you are alone, just simply start talking out loud to yourself and relate each sentence you speak in some way to the one before it. The sum of what you say doesn't have to make sense at all. If every sentence relates to the previous one, then you are doing it right. It's not as easy as you might think to do this without having to stop and think about what to say next. Try it.

This game might sound strange or pointless, but it is actually a very useful tool for practicing your social skills. A conversation between two people is actually very similar to this word game. One person says something, and the other person might ask them a question about what they said. They may also use what the other person said and perhaps relate it to something they've experienced in their own life. A naturally flowing conversation is almost always structured in this way. Until someone changes the topic, everything that is said is usually related in some way to what was previously said. Because this is the nature of conversations between two or more people, this word game will actually strengthen your ability to carry on a naturally flowing conversation with people. And you don't even have to leave your house!

There are other similar word games you can play as well, but I thought I would just give you this one to experiment with for now. If you want to make it really fun, you could play it with someone you know and see who can say the most sentences without stopping. You could make up your own word game as well. Whatever you decide to do, just remember that you have the ability to significantly improve your social skills using this tool if you choose to.

If you practice the things mentioned in this chapter, you will slowly build more confidence in your ability to navigate through the social world. If you are shy or have social anxiety, then you probably have low confidence when it comes to interacting with other people or large groups. When boiled down, the real underlying cause for your shyness and social anxiety is your lack of confidence. If you increase your confidence, you will naturally reduce your shyness and social anxiety, and the methods described in this chapter are designed to do just that.

Facing Fear and Expanding Your Comfort Zone

The previous chapters were designed to give you the necessary tools for increasing your confidence and social skills without actually having to go out and socialize with anyone. Following the methods described in those chapters will certainly improve your life, but the most drastic changes will occur when you get out of your comfort zone and socialize with as many people as you possibly can. This can be very scary for someone who suffers from social anxiety or extreme shyness, so I have designed this chapter in a way that will give you a step by step guide for easing into the social world and practicing your social skills.

Slowly adjusting yourself to certain social situations is the best way to improve without destroying your self-esteem or optimism. The key is to live on the *edge* of your comfort zone. This is where personal growth occurs. If you were to just throw yourself into the most stressful situation possible, you would risk coming out of it even less confident and shyer than before. Use this chapter as a guide for adjusting yourself to the social world. If you follow the steps, you will slowly transform yourself into a confident and outgoing person who is capable of handling challenges with ease. Here is a step by step method for increasing your confidence in social situations:

1. As you go throughout your day, make an effort to smile at everyone you see while also making steady eye contact. Don't feel pressured to say anything, just simply look people in the eyes and smile. Do this with *everyone*. This alone will increase your confidence greatly. By forcing yourself to make eye contact and

hold it until the other person looks away, you are sending a message to your brain that says 'I'm confident.' Smiling at people will give them the impression that you are a good person and are approachable. You will be amazed at the number of people that actually start a conversation with you simply because you gave them a smile. Do this one simple thing every day until it become easy and natural for you, then move on to the next step.

2. Now that you have gotten used to making eye contact and greeting people with your smile, you can take it a step further by greeting everyone with a "hello." Say 'hello' or 'hi' to every person who holds eye contact with you for more than a second. Still, there is no need to start a conversation, but saying hello will give the other person an invitation to do so if they wish. Practice doing this until it

becomes a habit, then follow the next step to continue making progress.

3. You should now be smiling, making eye contact, and saying hello to multiple people every single day. Your confidence should be growing and you should naturally feel more capable of meeting people. Now, your objective is to start asking at least three strangers every day how their day is going. Family or people you work with don't count. You must get used to approaching people and initiating conversation. If someone happens to make eye contact with you and smile, immediately say hello and ask the person how their day is going. From there, attempt to continue the conversation, but don't feel pressured to stay and chat for any certain amount of time. If the conversation has died or you feel extremely uncomfortable, just tell the person you have to leave. Initiate at least 3 conversations in this fashion every day.

Something this simple will allow you to meet many interesting people, some of which may become lifetime friends. Continue doing this until you have created the habit of talking to three strangers every day.

4. You should now be ready for some major changes. If you've done the three previous steps and are completely comfortable with them, then your confidence should be quite a bit higher compared to when you started. At this point, there are many different things that you could do to push yourself even further. Let me give you a few ideas:

-Randomly start conversations with members of the opposite sex.

-Take a public speaking class or join a mastermind group.

-Sing karaoke, even if you can't sing.

-Play practical jokes on complete strangers (nothing too crazy).

-Ask random questions to complete strangers.

The key to becoming confident and outgoing in social situations is to continuously throw yourself into situations that are slightly uncomfortable. When doing this, you will come face to face with your insecurities, you will face rejection, and you will not always have fun, but the reward for your willingness to persist through the pain is far better than you could imagine. Every time you face a situation that is uncomfortable, you evolve slightly. Facing your fears is the only way to overcome them. The more you can force yourself to leave your comfort zone, the faster you are going to increase your confidence and decrease your social anxiety. If you continue to do this, there is no limit to how far you can go. You will begin to see a brand new person evolve, and watching that process will be absolutely thrilling! There are not many things that compare to the feeling you get when you overcome challenges that you once thought were impossible to overcome. The journey will not be easy, but it will be worth it.

I think it is important to also understand that the journey of overcoming your shyness and social anxiety is not just about becoming better socially. More so, it is about becoming better at *life*! Overcoming your fears and increasing your confidence is going to benefit you in practically every aspect of your life. You will have better relationships, better health, more happiness, and greater success. Your life is far too valuable to waste it in a constant state of fear and anxiety. There are great things out there in the world for you to experience, and there will be challenges for you to overcome, but just know that every time you conquer an obstacle in your life, no matter how small, you become a stronger person because of it. Every challenge you overcome increases your ability to overcome even greater challenges, and before you know it, you will be living the life you always dreamed of.

As Albert Einstein once said, "Nothing happens until something moves." I want you to keep this in mind as you go on your journey of self-improvement, because there will be times when you sit and daydream about what you want from life, but none of those dreams will ever come true until you take action. You can read this book and understand the concepts, but that alone will not change your life. Apply these concepts to your life and practice them regularly. If you do that, you *will* see major positive change begin to happen. All is possible with a strong enough will and a burning desire. Keep in mind the person you want to become, and then consistently take the actions necessary to become that person. Be persistent, and you will get there.

Thank you so much for reading this book. I truly hope it supports you on your journey to the bigger and better things that you deserve.

If you enjoyed this book, please leave a review on Amazon. Your support means the world to me.

You can find more extremely helpful information (lots of FREE stuff) at healthandhappinessfoundation.com and my youtube channel, which you can find at BeauNorton.com

Made in the USA
Columbia, SC
16 January 2020

86863285R00030